OPTIMIZE VIDEO

E Crafting compelling and keyword-rich titles is crucial. Titles should be concise, engaging, and include relevant keywords for search optimization.

P Use tools like Google Keyword Planner to find relevant keywords. Ensure titles are attention-grabbing and accurately represent the video content.

I Improves discoverability and click-through rates.

1

CREATE HIGH-QUALITY THUMBNAILS

E Thumbnails serve as the first impression. Design eye-catching, high-resolution thumbnails that accurately represent the video content.

P Use graphic design tools or YouTube's thumbnail creator. Test different designs to see what resonates with your audience.

I Increases click-through rates and attracts viewers.

2

WRITE COMPELLING DESCRIPTIONS

E Provide detailed video descriptions with relevant keywords. Include links, timestamps, and a call-to-action to encourage engagement.

P Write a concise summary of the video content. Include links to related videos, social media, and a subscribe link.

I Enhances search visibility and promotes user engagement.

UTILIZE TAGS EFFECTIVELY

E Tags help YouTube understand the context of your video. Use a mix of broad and specific tags related to your content.

P Include relevant tags that describe the video content accurately. Use tools like TubeBuddy or VidIQ for tag suggestions.

I Improves search ranking and helps in suggested video recommendations.

CREATE PLAYLISTS

E Group related videos into playlists. This encourages users to watch more of your content, increasing overall watch time.

P Organize videos into playlists based on themes or topics. Feature playlists on your channel homepage.

I Boosts overall watch time and keeps viewers on your channel longer.

ENGAGE WITH YOUR AUDIENCE

Respond to comments, ask questions, and encourage viewers to share their thoughts. Building a community fosters a loyal audience.

P

Regularly monitor and respond to comments. Ask for feedback and create a sense of community.

I

Builds a dedicated audience and encourages repeat viewership.

UPLOAD CONSISTENTLY

E Consistency is key on YouTube. Establish a regular upload schedule to keep your audience engaged and anticipating new content.

P Create a content calendar and stick to a consistent uploading schedule (e.g., weekly, bi-weekly). Inform your audience about your posting schedule.

I Builds anticipation, keeps viewers engaged, and improves channel visibility.

COLLABORATE WITH OTHER YOUTUBERS

E Collaborations expose your channel to new audiences. Partner with other creators in your niche for joint projects or shoutouts.

P Identify potential collaborators with similar audience demographics. Reach out with a personalized collaboration proposal.

I Expands your reach and introduces your channel to new viewers.

CROSS-PROMOTE ON SOCIAL MEDIA

Share your YouTube videos on various social media platforms to reach a broader audience. Use platforms like Instagram, Twitter, and Facebook to promote your content.

Craft engaging posts with snippets or highlights from your videos. Use relevant hashtags and encourage sharing.

Drives traffic to your YouTube channel, increases exposure, and attracts new subscribers.

OPTIMIZE VIDEO LENGTH

Consider your audience's preferences and the nature of your content when determining video length. Aim for a balance between providing value and retaining audience attention.

P

Analyze your audience retention analytics. Test different video lengths and formats to find the optimal duration for your content.

Maintains viewer interest, improves watch time, and positively impacts search rankings.

CREATE COMPELLING INTROS

E Capture viewer attention within the first few seconds of your video. An engaging intro sets the tone for the content and encourages viewers to stay.

P Design a visually appealing intro with music and a brief preview of the video content. Keep it concise and relevant.

I Reduces viewer drop-off rates and increases the likelihood of video completion.

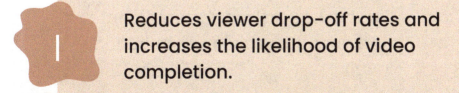

OPTIMIZE CHANNEL ART AND ABOUT SECTION

E A well-branded channel creates a professional image. Ensure your channel banner, logo, and about section accurately represent your content and personality.

P Use consistent branding elements in your channel art. Write a compelling 'About' section that introduces yourself and your channel's focus.

I Establishes a strong brand identity and encourages viewer trust and loyalty.

HOST GIVEAWAYS AND CONTESTS

E Running giveaways or contests encourages audience participation and can attract new subscribers. Offer relevant prizes related to your content.

P Clearly communicate the entry rules in your video and across your social media platforms. Use tools to randomly select winners and announce them in a follow-up video.

I Boosts engagement, attracts new viewers, and creates a buzz around your channel.

13

MONITOR ANALYTICS AND TRENDS

Regularly analyze YouTube Analytics to understand what works for your channel. Stay informed about trending topics in your niche.

P

Review audience demographics, watch time, and traffic sources. Use tools like Google Trends to identify trending topics in your niche.

Informs content strategy, helps refine targeting, and capitalizes on trending topics for increased visibility.

OPTIMIZE VIDEO END SCREENS

E Utilize end screens to keep viewers on your channel. Promote other videos, encourage subscriptions, and provide external links.

P Add end screens with links to related videos, playlists, or encourage subscriptions. Use a compelling call-to-action.

I Increases viewer retention and encourages additional views and interactions.

MASTER SEO TECHNIQUES

 E Understand and implement search engine optimization (SEO) principles to enhance your video's discoverability on YouTube.

 P Research relevant keywords, use them in titles, descriptions, and tags. Write detailed, keyword-rich video descriptions.

 **I** Improves search rankings, increases visibility, and attracts organic traffic.

HOST LIVE Q&A SESSIONS

E Live sessions foster real-time interaction with your audience. Host Q&A sessions to answer questions, share insights, and connect with your viewers.

P Announce the live session in advance. Encourage viewers to submit questions beforehand and during the live stream.

I Strengthens community engagement, builds a personal connection, and increases live view counts.

CREATE COMPELLING END SCREENS

E End screens are the last chance to engage your audience. Include elements like video links, subscribe buttons, and featured playlists.

P Use YouTube's end screen editor to add elements that encourage further interaction. Test different configurations to see what works best.

I Encourages additional views, subscriptions, and promotes deeper engagement with your content.

CREATE EYE-CATCHING CHANNEL TRAILERS

E A channel trailer is often the first thing new visitors see. Craft a compelling trailer that introduces your content and encourages subscriptions.

P Keep it short, engaging, and highlight the best aspects of your channel. Update it periodically to reflect changes in your content or style.

I Increases the likelihood of new visitors subscribing to your channel.

IMPLEMENT CARD ANNOTATIONS

E Use YouTube's card annotations to direct viewers to other relevant videos, playlists, or external links during a video.

P Add cards strategically throughout your video, promoting related content or encouraging subscriptions. Ensure they don't disrupt the viewing experience.

I Increases interaction, promotes additional views, and enhances user engagement.

PARTICIPATE IN YOUTUBE COMMUNITIES

E
Join and engage with YouTube and niche-specific communities. Contribute valuable insights and share your videos when appropriate.

P
Find relevant communities on YouTube, Reddit, or other platforms. Participate genuinely in discussions and avoid spamming your content.

I
Builds relationships with other creators and potential viewers, expanding your channel's reach.

OPTIMIZE MOBILE VIEWING EXPERIENCE

E Many users watch YouTube on mobile devices. Ensure your videos are mobile-friendly with readable text, clear visuals, and optimized formatting.

P Test your videos on various mobile devices. Use subtitles for accessibility and to cater to users watching without sound.

I Appeals to a broader audience and improves overall user satisfaction.

DIVERSIFY CONTENT TYPES

 E Experiment with different types of content to appeal to a wider audience. Mix in tutorials, vlogs, reviews, or other formats related to your niche.

 P Monitor audience reactions to different content types. Use YouTube analytics to identify popular video formats.

 **I** Attracts a diverse audience, increases watch time, and keeps your content fresh and interesting.

RUN PAID ADVERTISING CAMPAIGNS

E Utilize YouTube Ads to promote your videos to a targeted audience. Invest in campaigns to increase visibility and attract new subscribers.

P Define your target audience and set a budget for advertising campaigns. Monitor performance and adjust targeting based on results.

I Expands your channel's reach, introduces your content to new viewers, and boosts overall visibility.

UTILIZE ENDORSEMENTS AND TESTIMONIALS

E Seek endorsements or testimonials from satisfied viewers or influencers in your niche. Feature these in your videos or channel page.

P Reach out to satisfied viewers or collaborate with influencers for testimonials. Use positive quotes or clips in your content.

I Builds credibility, establishes trust, and can attract new viewers based on recommendations.

CREATE COMPELLING CHANNEL WATERMARKS

 Add a branded watermark to your videos, encouraging viewers to subscribe. Ensure it's unobtrusive but easily noticeable.

P Use YouTube's branding settings to add a watermark to your videos. Design it to match your channel's branding.

 Increases subscription rates and serves as a constant reminder for viewers to subscribe.

OPTIMIZE VIDEO TRANSCRIPTS

E Provide accurate transcripts for your videos. This not only aids accessibility but also improves search engine understanding of your content.

P Manually transcribe your videos or use automated tools. Add the transcript to your video description.

I Enhances search engine optimization, increases accessibility, and attracts a wider audience.

RUN SPECIAL EVENTS OR SERIES

 E Plan special events or series on your channel. This could be a themed month, special interviews, or unique challenges.

 **P** Promote the event or series in advance. Create a playlist or dedicated section on your channel.

I Generates excitement, encourages viewers to return for specific content, and can lead to increased subscriber loyalty.

ENCOURAGE USER-GENERATED CONTENT

E Invite your audience to create content related to your channel. Feature the best submissions in your videos or on your channel.

P Clearly communicate the guidelines for submissions. Create a dedicated hashtag for users to use when sharing their content.

I Fosters a sense of community, increases engagement, and provides fresh, diverse content for your channel.

MONITOR AND RESPOND TO TRENDS

E Stay informed about current trends and incorporate them into your content when relevant. This can attract attention from broader audiences.

P

Regularly check trending topics on YouTube and other social media platforms. Create content that aligns with popular trends.

I Increases the likelihood of your videos appearing in search and recommendation algorithms, attracting new viewers.

CAPITALIZE ON HOLIDAYS AND EVENTS

E Tailor your content to holidays, special occasions, or trending events. This can make your videos timely and relevant.

P Create themed content around holidays or events. Plan in advance to ensure timely release.

I Expands your reach during specific periods, taps into seasonal interests, and increases shareability.

OPTIMIZE CHANNEL KEYWORDS

E Use relevant keywords in your channel description and metadata. This helps YouTube understand the focus of your channel.

P Research and incorporate keywords related to your niche in your channel description and metadata.

I Improves searchability, enhances the discoverability of your channel, and attracts a targeted audience.

LEVERAGE COMMUNITY TAB

E If eligible, use the Community tab to share updates, polls, and exclusive content with your subscribers. This increases engagement between video uploads.

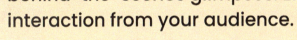

P Regularly update the Community tab with relevant content, questions, or behind-the-scenes glimpses. Encourage interaction from your audience.

I Fosters a sense of community, keeps your audience engaged between videos, and increases overall channel activity.

CREATE COMPELLING CHANNEL TRAILERS

E — A well-crafted channel trailer is essential for attracting new subscribers. Make it concise, engaging, and reflective of your channel's content.

P — Capture the essence of your channel in a short video. Include highlights, your value proposition, and a clear call-to-action.

I — Encourages new visitors to subscribe, provides a quick overview of your content, and sets the tone for your channel.

PROMOTE EXCLUSIVE CONTENT FOR SUBSCRIBERS

E Offer exclusive content, such as behind-the-scenes footage, early access, or special discounts, to your subscribers. This incentivizes viewers to subscribe.

P Clearly communicate the exclusive benefits of subscribing in your videos and channel description. Deliver on the promised exclusive content.

I Increases subscriber loyalty, provides added value, and can attract new subscribers who want access to exclusive content.

OPTIMIZE VIDEO PUBLISHING TIMES

E Identify the peak times when your audience is most active. Schedule your video uploads during these times to maximize initial engagement.

P Analyze your YouTube Analytics to determine when your audience is online. Experiment with different publishing times and monitor performance.

I Increases the likelihood of immediate engagement, improving video visibility and overall performance.

HOST VIRTUAL EVENTS

E Take your engagement to the next level by hosting virtual events like webinars, live workshops, or online Q&A sessions. This allows for real-time interaction with your audience.

P Promote the event across your social media platforms and on your channel. Use live chat features for direct interaction during the event.

I Creates a unique and immersive experience, fosters real-time connection, and encourages live participation.

UTILIZE INTERACTIVE CARDS

Leverage YouTube's interactive cards feature to add polls, quizzes, or links to related content directly within your videos. This boosts viewer engagement.

P

Insert interactive cards at strategic points in your videos. Create engaging polls or quizzes related to your content.

Enhances viewer interactivity, extends watch time, and provides valuable insights into audience preferences.

EXPERIMENT WITH CINEMATIC STORYTELLING

E Elevate the production value of your videos by incorporating cinematic storytelling techniques. This involves creative camera angles, compelling narratives, and high-quality editing.

P Invest time in scripting and storyboarding your videos. Experiment with cinematic techniques such as dynamic camera movement and creative editing.

I Captivates viewers with visually stunning content, sets your channel apart, and attracts a broader audience.

COLLABORATE IN UNIQUE WAYS

Go beyond standard collaborations by exploring unique partnership ideas. This could involve joint projects, challenges, or even co-hosting content with creators from different niches.

Brainstorm creative collaboration ideas that align with both your and the partner's audience. Ensure the collaboration feels authentic and adds value.

Expands your audience to new niches, creates cross-promotional opportunities, and generates excitement among viewers.

CREATE INTERACTIVE END-OF-YEAR REVIEWS

E Summarize your channel's highlights and milestones at the end of each year in an interactive and engaging format. Ask viewers for their favorite moments and memories.

P Compile a highlight reel of your best content and achievements throughout the year. Encourage viewers to share their favorite moments in the comments or through polls.

I Fosters a sense of community reflection, showcases your channel's growth, and encourages engagement during the year-end period.

IMPLEMENT AUGMENTED REALITY (AR) ELEMENTS

E Experiment with AR elements in your videos to add a layer of interactivity. This could involve virtual objects, effects, or even AR games related to your content.

P Explore AR tools and apps that integrate with video editing software. Design creative and relevant AR elements to enhance viewer experience.

I Adds a cutting-edge and interactive element to your content, making it more shareable and memorable.

HOST VIRTUAL REALITY (VR) EXPERIENCES

E Dive into the world of virtual reality by creating immersive VR content. This can include virtual tours, experiences, or storytelling in a VR environment.

 **P** Invest in VR equipment and software compatible with YouTube VR. Design content that leverages the unique aspects of VR technology.

 **I** Differentiates your content, provides an innovative viewing experience, and taps into the growing interest in virtual reality.

DEVELOP A BRANDED MOBILE APP

E Extend your brand beyond YouTube by creating a mobile app that offers exclusive content, community features, or even mini-games related to your channel.

P Work with app developers to create a user-friendly app. Integrate features that complement your YouTube content. Promote the app on your channel.

I Expands your brand presence, offers a dedicated space for your community, and provides an additional channel for content delivery.

44

HOST VIRTUAL FAN MEETUPS

E

Bring your community together by organizing virtual fan meetups. This could involve live video sessions, Q&A sessions, or exclusive announcements for your most dedicated viewers.

P

Plan and promote the virtual meetup in advance. Use live streaming or video conferencing platforms to facilitate the interaction.

I

Strengthens the bond with your audience, recognizes and rewards loyal viewers, and fosters a sense of belonging within your community.

LAUNCH LIMITED EDITION MERCHANDISE

E Create a sense of exclusivity by offering limited edition merchandise tied to specific milestones, anniversaries, or events related to your channel.

P Design unique and high-quality merchandise. Clearly communicate the limited availability and promote it in your videos and on social media.

I Generates excitement among your audience, provides additional revenue streams, and creates a sense of urgency to engage with your content.

EXPLORE 360-DEGREE VIDEO CONTENT

E Engage your audience with immersive 360-degree videos that allow viewers to control their perspective. This is especially effective for content related to travel, exploration, or unique environments.

P Use a 360-degree camera to capture your content. Edit and upload the video using YouTube's 360-degree video support.

I Enhances viewer immersion, provides a unique viewing experience, and sets your content apart from traditional formats.

47

CREATE CHOOSE-YOUR-ADVENTURE VIDEOS

E Turn your videos into interactive experiences by incorporating choose-your-adventure elements. Viewers can make decisions that impact the direction of the storyline.

P Plan branching storylines and choices within your video. Use YouTube's interactive features or external tools to create clickable choices.

I Increases viewer engagement, encourages multiple viewings, and provides an innovative and participatory viewing experience.

CREATE INTERACTIVE SOCIAL MEDIA CHALLENGES

E Develop and promote challenges on platforms like Instagram, Twitter, or TikTok that are tied to your YouTube content. Encourage your audience to participate and share their entries.

P Design challenges that align with your content and encourage creativity. Use branded hashtags to track entries and create a sense of community.

I Generates buzz on multiple platforms, increases visibility, and draws in a wider audience through user-generated content.

COLLABORATE WITH NICHE-SPECIFIC INFLUENCERS

E Identify influencers within your niche who are not directly competitive but share a similar audience. Collaborate on cross-promotional content or shout-outs.

P Reach out to influencers with a personalized collaboration proposal. Ensure that the collaboration adds value to both audiences.

I Leverages the existing audience of influencers, introduces your channel to a new demographic, and builds credibility within your niche.

UTILIZE ALTERNATIVE SOCIAL PLATFORMS

E Explore emerging or niche social platforms that align with your content. For example, platforms like Discord, Clubhouse, or Reddit can offer unique promotion opportunities.

P Create and engage with communities on alternative platforms. Share exclusive content or behind-the-scenes insights related to your YouTube channel.

I Expands your online presence, reaches audiences beyond traditional platforms, and taps into niche communities.

51

HOST VIRTUAL PREMIERE EVENTS

 **E** Generate excitement around your video releases by hosting virtual premiere events. This allows you to chat with viewers in real-time before the video starts.

P Schedule premiere events for your video releases. Encourage viewers to join the premiere, ask questions, and interact with you.

 **I** Creates anticipation for new content, increases live engagement, and fosters a sense of community around your video releases.

LEVERAGE QR CODES IN OFFLINE MARKETING

E Incorporate QR codes in your offline promotional materials, such as business cards, posters, or merchandise. When scanned, these codes can direct individuals to your YouTube channel.

P Create visually appealing QR codes linked to your channel. Include them on physical promotional materials or even in-store displays.

I Bridges the gap between offline and online promotion, provides a seamless way for people to discover your channel, and enhances overall brand visibility.

HOST CROSS-PLATFORM GIVEAWAYS

E Collaborate with creators on different platforms (e.g., Instagram, Twitter, or TikTok) for cross-platform giveaways. Participants may need to follow you on multiple platforms for entry.

P Coordinate with collaborators for a cohesive giveaway. Clearly communicate the entry requirements and deadlines across all participating platforms.

I Increases your visibility across various platforms, attracts diverse audiences, and fosters collaboration with creators from different communities.

IMPLEMENT VIRTUAL REALITY (VR) TUTORIALS

E Dive into the world of virtual reality by creating tutorials or experiences that provide hands-on learning in a VR environment. This is especially effective for content related to skills, art, or education.

P Invest in VR equipment and software compatible with YouTube VR. Develop immersive tutorials that take advantage of the 3D space.

I Offers a unique and immersive learning experience, sets your content apart, and appeals to audiences interested in innovative educational approaches.

55

CREATE CINEMATIC MINI-SERIES

E Elevate your storytelling by creating a cinematic mini-series on your channel. Break down a larger narrative into shorter, episodic segments, encouraging viewers to return for the next installment.

P Develop a cohesive storyline with engaging characters. Release episodes at consistent intervals, building anticipation for the next part.

I Increases viewer retention, encourages binge-watching, and builds a dedicated audience invested in your narrative content.

EXPERIMENT WITH ASMR STORYTELLING

E Explore ASMR (Autonomous Sensory Meridian Response) as a storytelling medium. Combine immersive storytelling with ASMR elements to create a unique and relaxing viewing experience.

P Research ASMR techniques and incorporate them into your storytelling. Experiment with whispering, ambient sounds, or tactile triggers that complement your narrative.

I Taps into the ASMR community, provides a soothing and distinctive viewing experience, and attracts a specific audience interested in relaxation content.

INTEGRATE AUGMENTED REALITY (AR) PRODUCT DEMONSTRATIONS

E Showcase products or concepts using augmented reality overlays. This allows viewers to interact with virtual elements in your real-world videos, enhancing the demonstration experience.

P Use AR tools to integrate virtual elements into your videos. Ensure that the AR additions are relevant and enhance the understanding of the demonstrated content.

I Provides an interactive and engaging product demonstration, showcases innovation, and appeals to tech-savvy audiences interested in AR experiences.

HOST COLLABORATIVE STORYTELLING PROJECTS

E Collaborate with your audience to create collaborative storytelling projects. Encourage viewers to contribute ideas, characters, or plot twists that you incorporate into your videos.

P Use social media, polls, or dedicated video comments to collect ideas from your audience. Integrate the contributed elements into your storytelling.

I Fosters a sense of community involvement, encourages audience engagement, and creates a unique and dynamic storytelling experience.

IMPLEMENT 360-DEGREE LIVE STREAMS

E Take live streaming to the next level by streaming in 360 degrees. This allows viewers to control their perspective during the live event, creating an immersive experience.

P Use a 360-degree camera and compatible live streaming tools. Plan interactive live events that benefit from the immersive 360-degree format.

I Offers a dynamic and engaging live streaming experience, encourages audience participation, and sets your live content apart from traditional streams.

60

IMPLEMENT THEME WEEKS OR MONTHS

E Dedicate specific weeks or months to a thematic focus on your channel. This could involve exploring a particular topic, style, or challenge during that designated period.

P Plan content in advance around the chosen theme. Announce the theme to your audience and consistently deliver content aligned with it throughout the designated time frame.

I Provides variety while maintaining a consistent theme, increases viewer anticipation, and fosters a sense of cohesion across your content.

CREATE A SIGNATURE SERIES

E Develop a signature series that becomes a staple on your channel. This could be a weekly series, unique challenges, or a recurring event that viewers can look forward to regularly.

P Identify a concept that resonates with your audience and aligns with your channel's niche. Plan and schedule these episodes consistently.

I Establishes a predictable schedule, builds viewer loyalty, and creates a recognizable and anticipated element within your content calendar.

EXPERIMENT WITH CONSISTENT AESTHETIC CHANGES

E Maintain consistency while keeping your content visually fresh by implementing regular aesthetic changes. This could involve updating your channel's color scheme, graphics, or intro/outro elements periodically.

P Design and implement aesthetic changes at planned intervals. Ensure these changes align with your brand and enhance the overall visual appeal of your channel.

I Keeps your channel visually interesting, demonstrates attention to detail, and provides a sense of evolution without straying from your core brand identity.

HOST CONSISTENT LIVE EVENTS

E Schedule regular live events on your channel, such as Q&A sessions, interviews, or interactive discussions. Consistency in these live sessions can become a regular engagement point for your audience.

P Establish a consistent schedule for live events. Promote upcoming sessions in advance to build anticipation. Interact with your audience during live broadcasts.

I Creates a predictable engagement opportunity, fosters real-time interaction, and encourages viewers to return for regularly scheduled live content.

IMPLEMENT A CONSISTENT CONTENT FORMAT

E Stick to a specific content format that sets your channel apart. This could be a unique editing style, storytelling technique, or presentation format that viewers can associate with your brand.

P Identify a content format that aligns with your channel's theme and resonates with your audience. Use this format consistently across your videos.

I Builds brand recognition, creates a cohesive viewing experience, and establishes a distinct identity for your channel.

CONSISTENT POSTING TIMES WITH A TWIST

E While consistent posting times are important, add a twist by occasionally surprising your audience with unexpected bonus content or impromptu releases. This keeps viewers on their toes while maintaining a regular schedule.

P Stick to your primary posting schedule but occasionally surprise your audience with extra content. Communicate these surprises on your social media channels.

I Enhances viewer engagement, adds an element of excitement, and reinforces the importance of consistency even when introducing surprises.

HOST VIRTUAL PREMIERE PARTIES

E
Turn your video premieres into virtual events by hosting premiere parties. Encourage your audience to join live chat during the premiere, and create a festive atmosphere with virtual celebrations.

P
Announce premiere parties on social media, build anticipation, and actively participate in the live chat during the premiere. Consider using themed emojis and interactive elements.

I
Enhances the premiere experience, boosts live engagement, and turns video releases into social events that attract more viewers.

RUN MYSTERY CONTENT TEASERS

E Generate excitement by creating teaser campaigns for upcoming content without revealing the full details. Use cryptic clues, snippets, or visual hints to build anticipation.

P Release teaser content across your social media platforms and YouTube. Encourage your audience to guess the theme or content of the upcoming video.

I Creates a sense of mystery and anticipation, encourages audience speculation, and generates curiosity that drives viewership.

HOST EXCLUSIVE LIVE SHOPPING EVENTS

E Combine live streaming with e-commerce by hosting exclusive live shopping events. Showcase products related to your channel, offer special promotions, and interact with viewers in real-time.

P Identify products or merchandise to feature. Promote the live shopping event on your channel and social media. Engage with viewers' questions and feedback during the live stream.

I Expands revenue streams, boosts product visibility, and creates an interactive shopping experience for your audience.

INTERACTIVE SCAVENGER HUNT CAMPAIGNS

E Create interactive scavenger hunt campaigns across your videos or social media platforms. Encourage viewers to find hidden clues, solve puzzles, or complete challenges to unlock exclusive content or discounts.

P Strategically place clues or challenges in your videos or social media posts. Announce the scavenger hunt campaign with clear instructions and incentives.

I Boosts engagement across multiple platforms, encourages audience interaction, and creates a fun and memorable promotional campaign.

UTILIZE AUGMENTED REALITY (AR) FILTERS FOR PROMOTION

E Develop and promote custom AR filters related to your channel. Encourage your audience to use these filters in their social media posts and tag your channel for a chance to be featured.

P Collaborate with AR developers to create branded filters. Announce the launch on your channel and encourage participation. Feature user-generated content with your AR filter.

I Expands your brand presence on social media, encourages user participation, and leverages the popularity of AR filters for promotional purposes.

CREATE LIMITED-EDITION COLLABORATIVE MERCHANDISE

E Collaborate with other creators or brands to create limited-edition merchandise. Release the exclusive products simultaneously on both channels, cross-promoting to each other's audiences.

P Collaborate with a creator or brand aligned with your content. Design and release limited-edition merchandise together, promoting it on both channels.

I Expands your audience through cross-promotion, boosts merchandise sales, and builds collaborative relationships within your content niche.

ENGAGE WITH YOUTUBE SHORTS

E Capitalize on the YouTube Shorts algorithm by creating short-form, vertical videos. Use engaging and attention-grabbing content to maximize visibility on the Shorts shelf.

P Create content specifically for YouTube Shorts. Utilize catchy thumbnails, add trending music, and include relevant hashtags. Monitor performance through YouTube Analytics.

I Increases visibility within the Shorts ecosystem, attracts a younger audience, and taps into the platform's focus on short-form content.

UTILIZE YOUTUBE CHAPTERS EFFECTIVELY

E Leverage YouTube's chapter feature by creating well-organized video chapters. This not only enhances user experience but can also positively impact algorithmic recommendations.

P Structure your videos with clear chapter markers. Use descriptive titles for each chapter. Encourage viewers to engage with specific chapters by asking questions or promoting key moments.

I Improves user engagement, enhances watch time, and signals to the algorithm the relevance of different sections within your videos.

INCORPORATE VIEWER INTERACTION TRIGGERS

E

Encourage specific viewer actions during your videos to boost engagement signals for the algorithm. This could include asking viewers to like, comment, share, or participate in polls.

P

Strategically place calls-to-action within your videos. Experiment with interactive elements like polls, annotations, or clickable links. Analyze engagement data to refine your approach.

I

Enhances viewer interaction, signals positive engagement to the algorithm, and increases the likelihood of video recommendations.

OPTIMIZE THUMBNAILS FOR CLICK-THROUGH RATE (CTR)

E Design eye-catching thumbnails that entice viewers to click on your videos. Test different thumbnail styles and elements to see what resonates best with your audience.

P Use bold and contrasting colors, readable text, and compelling imagery in your thumbnails. Analyze CTR data in YouTube Analytics and refine thumbnail designs based on performance.

I Improves the likelihood of your videos being clicked on, increases CTR, and positively influences algorithmic recommendations.

RUN VIEWER RETENTION EXPERIMENTS

E Experiment with different video structures, content formats, or hooks to see how they impact viewer retention. Higher retention rates signal to the algorithm that your content is engaging and valuable.

P Create variations of your videos, changing elements such as the introduction, pacing, or format. Analyze viewer retention data to identify successful experiments and incorporate findings into your content strategy.

I Improves video performance in algorithmic recommendations, as higher retention rates are a key factor in YouTube's recommendation algorithm.

IMPLEMENT STRATEGIC UPLOAD PATTERNS

E Test different upload patterns to understand how they impact your channel's performance. This could involve experimenting with upload frequency, days of the week, or specific times.

P Analyze YouTube Analytics to identify patterns in viewer activity. Experiment with different upload schedules and assess the impact on views, watch time, and subscriber growth.

I Optimizes the timing of your content for when your audience is most active, maximizing the initial engagement and increasing the likelihood of algorithmic recommendations.

UTILIZE YOUTUBE ANALYTICS INSIGHTS

E Dive deep into your YouTube Analytics to understand audience behavior. Identify top-performing videos, audience demographics, and traffic sources.

P Regularly review YouTube Analytics data to identify trends and patterns. Use insights to refine content strategy, target specific demographics, and optimize promotional efforts.

I Informs data-driven decision-making, allowing you to tailor content and promotion strategies for maximum impact on your target audience.

LEVERAGE YOUTUBE PREMIERE EVENTS

Utilize YouTube Premiere for scheduled video releases. This feature creates a live chat around your video premiere, boosting initial engagement.

Schedule your video release as a Premiere. Announce the Premiere on your social media and within your community. Engage with viewers in the live chat during the Premiere.

Enhances the initial visibility and engagement of your videos, signaling positive interaction to the algorithm.

OPTIMIZE VIDEO TITLES FOR SEARCH INTENT

E

Craft video titles that align with user search intent. Use relevant keywords and ensure your title accurately represents the content of your video.

P

Research relevant keywords using tools like Google Keyword Planner. Create titles that not only include keywords but also entice clicks. Monitor performance and refine titles based on search trends.

I

Improves discoverability by aligning your content with user search queries, leading to higher chances of appearing in search results and recommendations.

CREATE PLAYLISTS WITH THEMATIC GROUPING

E Organize your videos into playlists with a common theme or topic. This encourages viewers to watch multiple videos in one sitting, increasing overall watch time.

P Group related videos into playlists. Optimize playlist titles and descriptions. Feature playlists prominently on your channel.

I Boosts overall watch time, enhances user experience, and signals to the algorithm that your content is engaging and valuable.

IMPLEMENT AUDIENCE RETENTION STRATEGIES

E Focus on keeping viewers engaged throughout your videos. Optimize content pacing, use engaging visuals, and strategically place compelling moments.

P Monitor audience retention metrics in YouTube Analytics. Experiment with video editing techniques to maintain viewer interest. Analyze performance data and refine strategies accordingly.

I Higher audience retention indicates quality content to the algorithm, increasing the likelihood of your videos being recommended to a broader audience.

EXPLORE COLLABORATIVE PLAYLIST CREATION

E Collaborate with other creators to curate playlists featuring each other's content. This cross-promotional strategy benefits both channels by introducing audiences to related content.

P Reach out to creators in your niche for collaboration. Create and share collaborative playlists on your respective channels. Encourage viewers to explore the playlists for a curated content experience.

I Expands your reach through collaboration, increases cross-promotion opportunities, and introduces your audience to content from other creators.

PARTICIPATE IN YOUTUBE CHALLENGES

E Engage with trending challenges on YouTube. Whether it's a dance challenge, cooking challenge, or any other viral trend, participation can place your video on the radar of both viewers and the algorithm.

P Keep an eye on current challenges trending on YouTube. Create content that aligns with the challenge and incorporate relevant hashtags. Encourage your audience to participate as well.

I Positions your video within the trend, increasing visibility and making it more likely to appear on the Trending section.

LEVERAGE CURRENT EVENTS AND NEWS

E Create timely content related to current events, news, or trending topics. This can capitalize on the increased search and discovery related to ongoing discussions.

P Stay informed about current events in your niche or globally. Produce relevant content that adds value or provides a unique perspective. Release the content in a timely manner.

I Capitalizes on heightened search interest, increasing the likelihood of your video appearing in search results and the Trending section.

COLLABORATE ON TIMELY AND RELEVANT TOPICS

E Collaborate with other creators on videos related to current trends or events. This not only expands your reach but also increases the chances of your collaborative content trending.

P Identify creators who align with your content and are open to collaboration. Plan and execute collaborations around trending topics or challenges. Cross-promote the collaborative video on both channels.

I Leverages the combined audience of collaborators, increases visibility, and adds a collaborative element that can enhance trending potential.

CREATE UNIQUE AND SHAREABLE CONTENT

E Develop content that is not only high-quality but also highly shareable. Shareability increases the likelihood of your video being shared across social media platforms, contributing to trending potential.

P Focus on content that evokes strong emotions, educates, or entertains. Include calls-to-action encouraging viewers to share the video. Monitor and engage with social media shares.

I Increases the likelihood of your video being shared, reaching a wider audience, and potentially trending on YouTube.

UTILIZE HASHTAGS STRATEGICALLY

E Incorporate relevant and trending hashtags in your video descriptions. This can increase discoverability, especially if users are searching for or clicking on those specific hashtags.

P Research popular and relevant hashtags in your niche. Include them in your video descriptions to make your content discoverable when users search for or click on those hashtags.

I Enhances discoverability, making your video more likely to appear in searches and trend in relevant hashtag feeds.

CREATE 'HOW-TO' AND TUTORIAL CONTENT

E Produce high-quality 'how-to' or tutorial content that addresses common challenges or interests. People often search for instructional content, especially during trends or when new technologies emerge.

P Identify topics within your niche that can be addressed with 'how-to' or tutorial content. Create step-by-step guides or informative videos. Optimize titles and thumbnails for searchability.

I Positions your video as a valuable resource, increasing search visibility and the likelihood of appearing in the Trending section for relevant topics.

IMPLEMENT LANGUAGE-SPECIFIC PLAYLISTS

E Organize your videos into language-specific playlists. This makes it easier for viewers to find content in their preferred language and enhances the overall organization of your channel.

P Create playlists for each language you produce content in. Clearly label and describe the playlists in their respective languages. Promote these playlists on your channel homepage.

I Provides a seamless viewing experience for users who speak different languages, increases the visibility of language-specific content, and improves overall channel organization.

LEVERAGE YOUTUBE'S SUBTITLE FEATURE

E Utilize YouTube's automatic subtitles or provide manual translations for your videos. This enables viewers to access content in their preferred language, improving accessibility and global appeal.

P Enable automatic subtitles for your videos or upload manually translated subtitle files. Encourage your audience to contribute subtitles in different languages through YouTube's community contributions.

I Enhances accessibility for international viewers, improves SEO by making your content searchable in multiple languages, and attracts a more diverse audience.

COLLABORATE WITH MULTI-LANGUAGE CREATORS

E Collaborate with creators who produce content in different languages. This allows you to tap into their audience and introduce your content to viewers who speak those languages.

P Identify creators who produce content in languages you want to target. Propose collaborations that are mutually beneficial. Promote the collaborative content on both channels.

I Expands your audience across language barriers, creates cross-promotional opportunities, and introduces your content to new language-specific communities.

HOST MULTILINGUAL Q&A SESSIONS

E Conduct Q&A sessions where you answer questions in multiple languages. This interactive approach demonstrates your commitment to a diverse audience and engages viewers on a personal level.

P Collect questions from your audience in various languages. Schedule and announce multilingual Q&A sessions. Respond to questions in their respective languages.

I Builds a sense of inclusivity, strengthens connections with viewers who speak different languages, and showcases your commitment to a global audience.

CREATE LANGUAGE-SPECIFIC COMMUNITY POSTS

E Utilize YouTube's Community tab to share updates, polls, and exclusive content in different languages. This ensures that your entire audience can engage with your community posts.

P Write community posts in different languages, clearly labeling the language used. Use translation tools to assist if needed. Encourage interactions and responses in the language of the post.

I Fosters engagement from viewers across different language communities, creates a more inclusive online space, and strengthens the sense of community on your channel.

HOST VIRTUAL MULTILINGUAL EVENTS

E Conduct live events, such as webinars or live streams, where you communicate in multiple languages. This can be particularly engaging for a diverse audience.

P Plan and promote virtual events in advance. Clearly communicate the languages you'll be using. Encourage viewers to interact in the language of their choice.

I Creates an inclusive and dynamic live experience, accommodates viewers from different language backgrounds, and demonstrates cultural sensitivity.

HOST EXCLUSIVE SUBSCRIBER-ONLY CONTENT

E Incentivize subscriptions by offering exclusive content for your subscribers. This could include behind-the-scenes footage, early access to videos, or special Q&A sessions.

P Clearly communicate the benefits of subscribing for exclusive content. Regularly release subscriber-only videos. Promote the exclusivity on your channel and social media.

I Encourages more viewers to subscribe, boosts loyalty, and provides an added incentive for new and existing subscribers.

RUN LIMITED-TIME SUBSCRIBER CHALLENGES

E Create challenges or events specifically for your subscribers. For example, you could run a contest where subscribers can win exclusive merchandise or shout-outs.

P Announce the subscriber challenge with clear instructions and incentives. Promote the challenge across your social media and within your videos. Showcase winners and their submissions.

I Fosters engagement and participation from your subscribers, encourages new subscriptions, and creates a sense of community on your channel.

IMPLEMENT "SUBSCRIBE FOR A SURPRISE" CAMPAIGNS

E Tease surprise content or rewards that subscribers will receive once they hit a specific subscriber milestone. This creates excitement and motivates viewers to subscribe for the upcoming surprise.

P Set subscriber milestones (e.g., "Subscribe for a special video at 100k subscribers"). Promote the campaign in your videos and social media. Deliver the promised surprise once the milestone is reached.

I Creates anticipation and excitement around subscriber milestones, motivating viewers to subscribe and be part of the milestone celebration.

HOST INTERACTIVE "LIKE CHALLENGES"

E Encourage viewers to hit the like button for a specific goal, such as unlocking bonus content, releasing a special video, or reaching a certain number of likes for a charity donation.

P Clearly state the goal tied to the like button in your videos. Provide updates on progress and remind viewers to participate. Deliver on the promised content or action once the like goal is achieved.

I Boosts engagement and likes on your videos, involves viewers in channel activities, and turns likes into a participatory element.

CREATE "SHARE AND TELL" CAMPAIGNS

E Run campaigns where viewers are encouraged to share your videos on social media and tag your channel. Highlight and reward those who actively participate in sharing your content.

 **P** Announce the campaign with clear instructions and incentives. Feature shared content or shout-outs in your videos. Express gratitude for viewer participation.

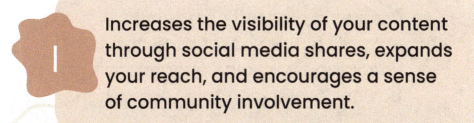 **I** Increases the visibility of your content through social media shares, expands your reach, and encourages a sense of community involvement.

IMPLEMENT "SUBSCRIBER OF THE MONTH" RECOGNITION

E Acknowledge and celebrate a "Subscriber of the Month" in your videos. This can include featuring their comments, giving them a shout-out, or even sending them personalized merchandise.

P Establish criteria for selecting the Subscriber of the Month. Announce and recognize the chosen subscriber in a dedicated video. Encourage viewers to engage for a chance to be featured.

I Creates a sense of community, rewards active subscribers, and encourages ongoing engagement to be considered for future recognition.

HOST LIVE SUBSCRIBER MILESTONE CELEBRATIONS

E Celebrate subscriber milestones in real-time during live streams. Engage with your audience, express gratitude, and celebrate collectively as a community.

P Announce upcoming live streams for subscriber milestones. Encourage your audience to subscribe and be part of the celebration. Interact with viewers in real-time during the live event.

I Creates a dynamic and interactive celebration, encourages subscribers to engage during live streams, and strengthens the sense of community on your channel.

RUN "SUBSCRIBER SHOUT-OUT" SESSIONS

E Dedicate sections of your videos to giving shout-outs to new subscribers. This personal touch can make viewers feel appreciated and encourage others to subscribe for a chance to be recognized.

P Allocate time in your videos for subscriber shout-outs. Highlight comments or channel names of new subscribers. Encourage viewers to comment after subscribing for a chance to be featured.

I Establishes a connection with your audience, acknowledges new subscribers, and incentivizes others to subscribe to receive recognition.

CREATE INTERACTIVE POLLS FOR VIDEO IDEAS

E Involve your audience in content creation by creating polls for video ideas. Allow subscribers to vote on topics or choose between different content options, making them feel more invested in your channel.

P Use YouTube's community tab or social media to create polls. Consider subscriber preferences when planning future content. Acknowledge and implement popular choices.

I Enhances viewer engagement, involves subscribers in content decisions, and increases the likelihood of likes and shares on videos that align with viewer preferences.

IMPLEMENT "SUBSCRIBE AND COMMENT" CONTESTS

E Run contests where viewers are required to subscribe and leave a comment for a chance to win prizes or be featured in your next video. This strategy encourages both subscription and engagement.

P Clearly communicate the contest rules and prizes. Monitor new subscriptions and comments. Announce winners and showcase their participation.

I Boosts engagement, encourages subscribers to take additional actions, and creates excitement around contests and giveaways.

CREATE "CHALLENGE ACCEPTED" SERIES

E Launch a series where you challenge your subscribers to participate in specific activities, whether it's recreating your content, sharing their stories, or showcasing their talents.

P Announce challenges in your videos and on social media. Feature submissions from participants in dedicated challenge videos. Acknowledge and reward standout entries.

I Fosters community involvement, encourages subscribers to actively participate, and generates user-generated content that can be shared and promoted.

RUN COLLABORATIVE "LIKE AND SHARE" CAMPAIGNS

E Collaborate with other creators to run joint "like and share" campaigns. Cross-promote each other's content, encouraging viewers to like, share, and subscribe to both channels.

P Partner with creators in your niche for joint campaigns. Clearly communicate the campaign goals and benefits. Cross-promote the collaborative content on both channels.

I Increases visibility through cross-promotion, encourages audience engagement, and creates a collaborative environment within your content niche.

www.ingramcontent.com/pod-product-compliance
Lightning Source LLC
La Vergne TN
LVHW051643050326
832903LV00022B/862